SandCastle™

Primeros Sonidos

Rita y Roberto

Cathy Camarena, M.Ed., and Gloria B. Ruff, M.Ed.

Consulting Editors

Lourdes Flores-Hanson, M.S.E., and Gloria Rosso-White

ABDO Publishing Company

capstone

www.capstoneclassroom.com

Rita y Roberto © 2006 by Abdo Consulting Group, Inc. International copyrights reserved in all countries. This version distributed and published by Capstone Classroom © 2016 with the permission of ABDO. No part of this book may be reproduced in any form without written permission from the publisher. SandCastle™ is a trademark and logo of ABDO Publishing Company.

Credits
Curriculum Coordinator: Nancy Tuminelly
Cover and Interior Design and Production: Mighty Media
Child Photography: Steven Wewerka, Wewerka Photography
Photo Credits: AbleStock, Corbis Images, Photodisc, Stockbyte

ISBN 978-1-4966-0367-8 (paperback)

Printed in the United States of America.
874

SandCastle™ books are created by a professional team of educators, reading specialists, and content developers around five essential components that include phonemic awareness, phonics, vocabulary, text comprehension, and fluency. All books are written, reviewed, and leveled for guided and early intervention reading, and designed for use in shared, guided, and independent reading and writing activities to support a balanced approach to literacy instruction.

SandCastle Level: Beginning

Rr

ABCChDEFGH
IJKLLLMNÑOP
QRSTUVWXYZ

abcchdefgh
ijklllmnñop
qrstuvwxyz

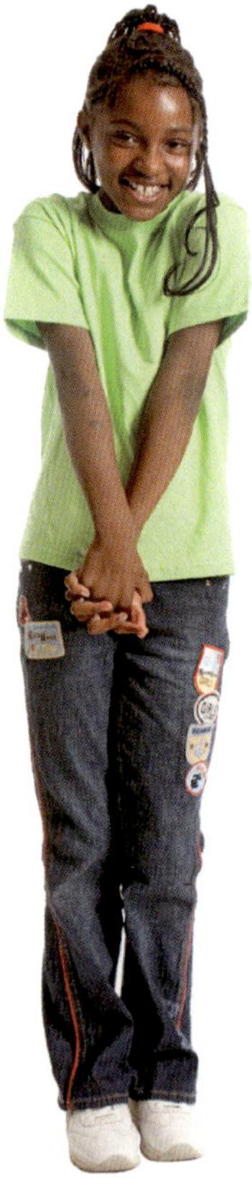

Rita

Roberto

rana

regalo

reloj

reina

rey

Es una  .

Es un  .

Es un  .

Ella es una .

Él es un  .

Roberto tiene un regalo.

El regalo tiene un lazo grande.

Rita tiene una rana.
La rana es verde.

La rana saltó
encima del regalo
de Roberto.

¿Cuáles de estas cosas comienzan con r?

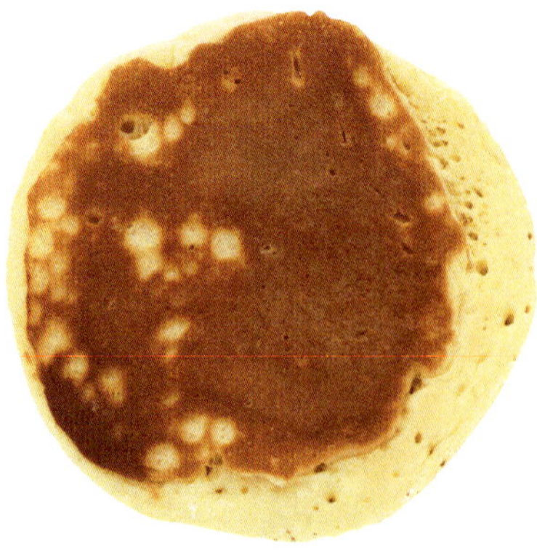

Más palabras que comienzan con r

rábano

radio

rastrillo

ratón

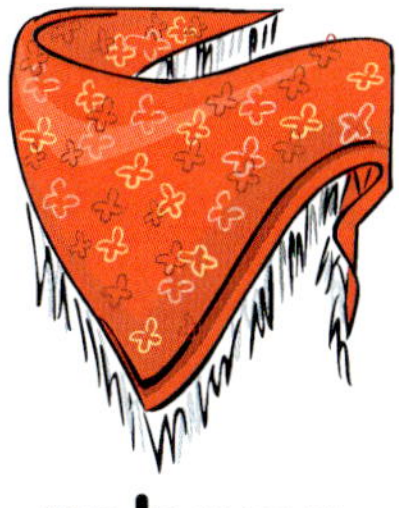

rebozo

About SandCastle™

A professional team of educators, reading specialists, and content developers created the SandCastle™ series to support young readers as they develop reading skills and strategies and increase their general knowledge. The SandCastle™ series has four levels that correspond to early literacy development in young children. The levels are provided to help teachers and parents select the appropriate books for young readers.

Emerging Readers
(no flags)

Beginning Readers
(1 flag)

Transitional Readers
(2 flags)

Fluent Readers
(3 flags)

These levels are meant only as a guide. All levels are subject to change.

ABDO Publishing Company

www.abdopub.com

capstone®

www.capstoneclassroom.com